CURIO NO. 6

YOU'VE NEVER HEARD YOUR FAVORITE SONG

100 DEEP CUTS TO MAKE YOUR WORLD SOUND BETTER

MATTHEW DOUCET

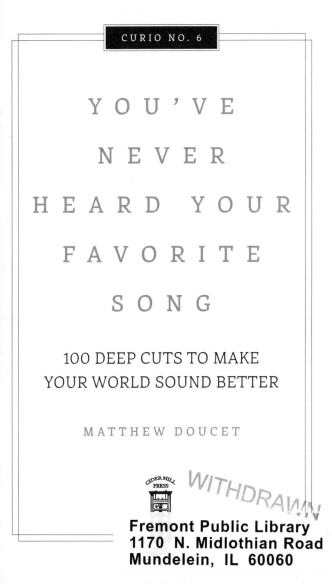

CIDER MILL PRESS

13-Digit ISBN: 978-1-60433-970-3
10-Digit ISBN: 1-60433-970-5

This book may be ordered by mail from the publisher. Please include $5.99 for
postage and handling. Please support your local bookseller first!
Books published by Cider Mill Press Book Publishers are available at special
discounts for bulk purchases in the United States by corporations, institutions, and
other organizations. For more information, please contact the publisher.

Cider Mill Press Book Publishers
"Where good books are ready for press"
PO Box 454
12 Spring Street
Kennebunkport, Maine 04046
Visit us online!
www.cidermillpress.com

Typography: Rival
Image Credits: All images used under official license from Shutterstock.com.

Printed in China
1 2 3 4 5 6 7 8 9 0
First Edition

CONTENTS

FOREWORD

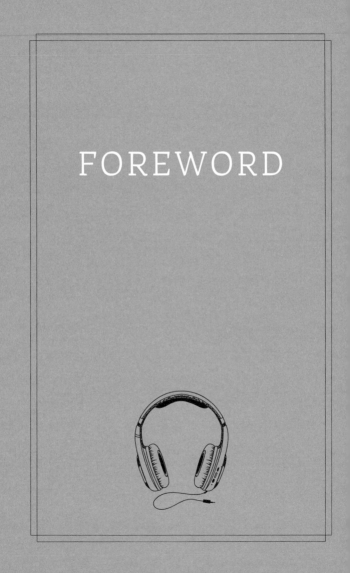

SONGS THAT ROCK (MINUS ONE)
by Jesse Jarnow

SOME DAYS, I want to peel the sticker off my laptop camera just so whatever entity is monitoring my screen can see me flip off the latest list of the top 100 greatest songs or albums from an artist or decade or scene. Get out of my face with these definitive tracks, these essential greatest hits that I need to hear before I die, like it's part of some checklist sequence that's already been initiated and I need to start making my final preparations before the inevitable.

You've Never Heard Your Favorite Song makes a more powerful argument and serves a higher task than a map or guidebook to genres, no matter how scholarly or well written. Certainly, it's a task more noble than a playlist spurted out by an algorithm, or even the most well-intentioned human curator down in the content mines. Instead, *You've Never Heard Your Favorite Song* is the territory itself, the entire world filled with all its music.

Presented with that elusive mix of historical context and evocative this-song-is-where-you-wanna-go-right-now lyricism, it's the kind of book that requires its own workflow. Though its page count might be slim, the entries constituting its content represent something far more elastic than their lengths might suggest. Some entries might take no more than a moment to glance over. But most won't, even if they're only one or two sentences.

At the most basic and obvious level, each has the potential—and the promise—to send you to your nearest WiFi-enabled celestial jukebox, expanding an entry at least to the duration of the track it describes. Probably you won't like all of them, and some might get switched off in a matter of a verse and a chorus (or even just the sound of a synth you can't stand). But there are those that might expand even further, into late-night internet searches, into raving texts to friends, into new musical realms.

There are some organizing principles, of course, and they appear in the mists like familiar points: Jamaican reggae, deep grooves from Africa, a section on earthy gospel. But these islands of familiarity are mirages, reference points to serve as constellations for space-time navigation.

You've Never Heard Your Favorite Song zig-zags across continents and decades, a kind of movement as literally fourth dimensional as one can access. There are no grand theses given, no particular logic offered for how it all connects, nor does the book feel lacking for their absence. At least in the consensual reality offered up by recorded music, there is already a shared timeline that stretches back to the beginning of recorded sound near the dawn of the 20th century, and a natural geography. All music is a pathway back to the cultures from which it came, and this book offers routes to a variety of highly specific destinations. Whether or not they know it, every music fan carries a combination atlas and family tree of how the music is connected, by sound or creator. Together, it all constitutes a set of shared coordinates for all music fans, and even non-music fans, an alternative world history in sound and song.

"There are other worlds they have not told you of," Saturnian jazz pioneer Sun Ra once intoned. *You've Never Heard Your Favorite Song* might hurl any music listener toward them, whether that listener is just starting to look for new pathways or is a seasoned music lifer. Without unnecessary horn-tootery, I'd like to think of myself as a fairly well-traveled listener with a broad knowledge of music across a variety of decades and some sense of how music history progressed on most continents. And still the song choices here threw me delightedly into new sound world after new sound world, often adjacent to ones I know, but not always.

I was casually familiar with around 20 of the artists featured here, but only two of the recordings. I'll only mention two of the songs that I've since fallen in love with from this book, because that's Matthew's job and I don't want to spoil what's to come, but my life is now richer for knowing the ethereal groove of Ozo's "Anambra," a 1976 12" from the Nigerian cosmic-disco frontier, and the beautiful Japanese folk of Gu's "Marianne," from 1970.

Being a book, it's necessarily a one-sided conversation, but likewise a very specific conversation. My friends and I used to play a road trip game called Songs That Rock, alternating picks, letting one suggest the next, and trying to create a continuous flow. *You've Never Heard Your Favorite Song*, then, is the Songs That Rock version of *Comedy Minus One*, the infamous 1973 Albert Brooks comedy LP that made room for home participation. The book is an invitation to enter the conversation in some way, perhaps via a friendly letter to the author, a social media post or two, or maybe just a new playlist on the device or platform or turntable of your choice. Maybe a silent conversation, never to be shared with anyone, chasing some private thread or sonic fingerprints across recordings.

Almost every song here provoked some kind of primal Songs That Rock reaction in my music-obsessed brain, what I might play next if a road trip companion served these up, and you might react similarly. At the risk of unduly highjacking Matthew's choices, I'll only throw out one, and a fairly lateral pick at that. Included here is "Normalizo," a percolating mid-'80s pop outing by South African expatriate Letta Mbulu. With which I counter: "I Need Your Love," an almost unbearably sweet soul cut from her 1970 album *Letta* arranged by the legendary Hugh Masekela.

The title of *You've Never Heard Your Favorite Song* is not a boast but a philosophy, a Zeno-like paradox for music heads. Your favorite song isn't waiting here. It's somewhere within reach, but you will never hear it, and you will never stop looking. For a music fan, that's not a threat, but a beautiful promise.

BROOKLYN, NY
NOVEMBER 2019

JESSE JARNOW is the author of *Wasn't That a Time: The Weavers, the Blacklist, & the Battle for the Soul of America* (Da Capo, 2018), *Heads: A Biography of Psychedelic America* (Da Capo, 2016), and *Big Day Coming: Yo La Tengo & the Rise of Indie Rock* (Gotham, 2012). He hosts the Frow Show on the freeform radio station WFMU and lives in Brooklyn.

INTRODUCTION

MANY OF THESE songs lay dormant for years. Others are lovingly tucked away in niches lacking the infrastructure to connect them with a larger audience. All are testaments to the dissonance between quality and recognition, despite the supposed genius of the market. Considering these realities, the amount of music that is produced and excavated every day, and the music that is forgotten and covered over by these arrivals, the seemingly bold declaration made by this book's title is nothing more than simple arithmetic, a nod to probability.

These songs have the urgency to shake you free from your programming, but are not themselves intended to bring your search to an end. Instead, they aim to make the title something of a mantra, spurring an avidity for other gems that have been pushed to the margins, and providing connections that will help you navigate the shadowy realm so much music is instantly relegated to. In there, everything matters. Each producer, session drummer, label, studio, and DJ who has previously provided you with something memorable is another point of light, a way to find a signal amid the pandemonium.

It is about more than discovering better music. It is a way to turn the world toward you, to play with the structures you were set down into until the unhelpful illusion of intrinsic personal integrity has dissolved. The prevailing aesthetics in the place you were born and the media your parents and friends exposed you to are inescapable influences. They are also far too powerful considering the narrow slices of the world they tend to stand upon. Music alone cannot forge an identity, but it is one of the least painful ways to discover that you may not be as in tune with your insides as you believe, and to discern which directions they wish to go.

Take the handful of songs that will face off against those to follow. Think of the moment when they attained a gravity that made them seem impossible—that they were in your life, that you'd ever managed to do without them. Part of the value of digging in is that you get to experience that exceptional feeling over and over. The other benefit—and perhaps the greater one—is what becomes of those songs that provide this feeling. Some will be supplanted by new discoveries. Some will be outright erased. But some, those that truly resonate, will retain every bit of their impact. Because you haven't had to go back and bother them for a fix. Because they've had the space to gather their energies. You may know every note. After a long period away, after countless encounters have carried you somewhere else, it feels like you're hearing them for the first time.

GOOD TIMES, BAD TIMES: R & B TO REGGAE

GLORIA ANN TAYLOR
LOVE IS A HURTING THING
(12" VERSION)
Selector Sound / 1976

A singer who will never record again, having been worn down by her controlling husband/producer and their flailing in the music business. A man desperate to save his career and his marriage, pinning his last few dollars on a long shot that has failed to come in for the better part of a decade.

When the record is finished, there is so little money left that it gets tossed into a sleeve better suited to convey portraits taken at Sears. A car containing the masters for the song and their entire label gets towed and is never seen again.

"Love Is a Hurting Thing" never should have reached any of us. And, had it started with anything other than that hair-curling guitar riff, there's a good chance that anyone who ever picked it up and put it on would have believed what the unfamiliar names and generic design suggested.

But Walter Whisenhunt, Gloria's husband and producer, managed to tap into the instincts that made him James Brown's right-hand man at one time. He saw that the shock of that guitar was strong enough to awaken anyone who encountered it, guaranteeing that the breezy orchestration and uncanny percussion he'd spent so much time on would get a fair hearing.

As with so many products born of desperation, the tune is near bursting. There's Browned-out guitars, an orchestra's worth of strings, pained stabs at a piano, percussion that veers from anxious to slinky. It could easily be too much, but each component is unique and accomplished enough that the final construction avoids feeling bloated and instead manages to capture the swirl of a relationship: uninhibited and anxious, uneven and repetitive, numbingly hollow, disturbingly acute. And all of this in the opening section.

When the time comes for Gloria to give her final vocal performance, she has the unenviable charge of hopping on a roller coaster at full speed, and she later admitted as much, saying, "I was afraid of 'Love Is A Hurting Thing' at the time because the music was so good and I didn't know if I could fit into it." That reticence is there, for a moment. But as she continues you can feel her gaining strength, spiking each line with warmth and pain and grit, putting more and more of herself into it until her story, the whole of it—the woman who was sent to an orphanage at 13, who gave birth to her first child at 16, who entrusted her heart and talent to the same man and watched him slowly dispose of both—has been set down.

DONNIE & JOE EMERSON
BABY
Enterprise & Co. / 1979

A small Washington town so seemingly innocuous it is named Fruitland. Two teenage brothers who produce ethereal, naive pop in a home studio that would be first-rate in New York or Los Angeles, never mind on a farm in a town with a population of 751. On their album cover, the brothers are mugging in outrageously collared white jumpsuits, flanked by Tiger Beat graphics. Their mentor and music teacher was one of the buglers at John F. Kennedy's funeral.

The setup carries a whiff of the Lynchian. Except the corresponding darkness never enters the narrative. Donnie and Joe Emerson's only window to the larger world was the pop music that came over the tractor's radio, and they submerged themselves in those songs until the far-off lands and lives that informed them seemed approachable, tangible. They then poured those daydreams into songs of their own, impressing their father enough that he took out a second mortgage on the house and invested $100,000 into building a studio.

Eventually, miraculously, that gamble proved to be worthwhile. The Emersons managed to produce an album, *Dreamin' Wild*, that has aged as well as anything coming out of America during the late '70s. Forging a sound that coolly internalized the tender soft rock of Laurel Canyon and the innocent heartbreak of doo-wop, while also anticipating the pointed hush of indie rock, *Dreamin' Wild* is proof that the Emersons' wonder enabled a fluency and vitality that sophistication had drilled out of their contemporaries.

"Baby" is the avatar of this triumph. Fittingly, the song sounds like it takes place within a dream: luminous, beautiful, a world that is compelling but likely inconsequential. The opening drums and piano are reminiscent of a teen scuffing down a street on a grey fall day, and the vocal is hesitant and mournful, charged with the inexperience that frames every frustration as a death, every delight as an arrival. It captures the youthful willingness to orbit around a vague feeling, reminding us of something we tend to excise from our recollections of adolescence: the considerable power of our feelings resulted more from the seriousness we affected in an attempt to provide ourselves some direction than the feelings themselves.

MICHAEL PROPHET
LOVE AND UNITY
Greensleeves Records / 1981

A worthy reggae rehabilitation center for those withered by repeated exposure to Bob Marley's *Legend* in their youth. Stemming from "Mash Down Rome," a production Michael Prophet made with his mentor, Yabby You, the fully fleshed out "Love and Unity" appears on Prophet's self-titled 1981 album. Untangling himself from the triumphant horns and bright, undulating percussion that made for two of Yabby's signatures, Prophet strips down the song to its anguished essence, leaving his tender voice to struggle against a drum that smacks of both hollowness and obduracy, a conflict the characteristically taut guitar and steadying bass are caught in the middle of.

Prophet sounds just weary enough that we understand this tenderness is not innate, but bred out of misfortune. A means of offering others the sympathy he suffered without, Prophet's gesture supplies the hope contained within the title, and avoids the glibness that typically attends such absolutes. He knows a world guided by love and unity is possible, and desirable. He also understands that it is unlikely. As the track winds down, he slowly recedes, an unsettling rattle taking his place, becoming as prominent as the echo of that constant, inflexible beat.

THIS MUST BE THE PLACE

The Napoleon of the music world: diminutive, seized by an unparalleled genius, author of a legacy that will reverberate for centuries. Four pathways into Jamaica's staggering tradition.

Tradition
The Breathtaking Blast
Venture Records / 1980

They kick off their sci-fi odyssey *Captain Ganja and the Space Control* with boundless space in every direction, making awe the only possible perspective. A startling testament to the power of dub.

Jackie Mittoo
Wall Street
Black Roots / 1981

Musical director at Jamaica's famed Studio One and mentor to numerous young artists, Mittoo's refracted tones on the organ gently slip the listener beneath the surface of a placid sea.

Willie Williams
Addis-A-Baba (Dub)
Studio One / 1979

The martial bass line of the Skatalites and
Coxsone Dodd's original remains intact on the
B side of this 1979 Studio One 7", but the horns
are toned down to clear space for an organ that
always remains just out of reach, no matter how
intently we strain to pull it in.

Dadawah
Run Come Rally
Wildflower / 1974

The track that won the series of coin flips to determine which one would represent his flawless 1974 album, *Peace and Love*. Sharper, fuller, and more urgent than what one expects from reggae, this has as much in common with the dark funk of Parliament-Funkadelic as it does with the other songs on this list.

JAN HAMMER GROUP
DON'T YOU KNOW
Nemperor Records / 1977

Yes, that Jan Hammer. Of *Miami Vice* fame. Purveyor of a sound so dated that even jokes made at its expense are tired.

I first came upon this in the middle of an Eric Duncan* mix that was much needed in the desolation that is winter in northern New Hampshire. Initially I thought, "Christ, this guy's got unreleased Stevie Wonder tracks." Then I saw it was the Jan Hammer Group, and realized ignorance and attitude, not access, had kept me from it previously.

-----

*Half of the scene-defining NYC DJ duo Rub N Tug, Duncan has used his taste, appetite for the good life, and genius for arrangement to build his enviable legacy. His edit of Edwin Starr's "Get Up Whirlpool" is not for everyone, but I wish we lived in a world where it was.

Fernando Saunders's proficiency on the bass made him an essential piece of numerous Hamilton Bohannon and Lou Reed projects, but this song reveals he easily could have spent his career in the foreground. The Wonder-ish tone of his vocal is perfect for lyrics that could easily become cringy, as he grants the gooey bromides and rebirth metaphors the weight they carry when shared between two happy people.

Hammer does everything else in this song that is a rare combination of tenderness and power. The calm but strong drumbeat; the muscular, burbling bass line that sets the bed for darting, crepuscular synths; the joyful lark on the Fender Rhodes; the sun-drenched strings—all flow out of Hammer's mind, shaping the song into something that manages to be ecstatic without also seeming slight or shallow. By the time the second verse arrives and the backing vocals kick in you are soaring, reveling in the sheer ability to appreciate another, to be able to believe in the possibility of something grander than yourself.

"Don't You Know" also provides a valuable principle to the musically curious: do not categorically dismiss an artist who reached a pinnacle that turned out to be on shaky ground. Hammer may be inextricable from the '80s, but he had a wildly impressive run in the '70s, turning out a number of timeless and innovative tunes with John McLaughlin's Mahavishnu Orchestra (his piano work on the meditative "You Know You Know" in particular), alongside percussion virtuoso David Earle Johnson (check out "Juice Harp" off the *Time Is Free* album), and with his own group.

That said, make sure you get the version of "Don't You Know" included on 1977's *Melodies*— there's a version on 1994's *Drive* where Hammer, still reeling from the excesses of the era when he became a household name, carries his creation dangerously close to the realms of Muzak.

LETTA MBULU
NORMALIZO
Munjale / 1983

In exchange for the solace they can provide, we allow past and place to have their way with us. Based on what suits the moment, our memories become either humbler or more elaborate than reality is capable of being. We look to the city when we have grown stale in the open country, the country when burnt out by the city's fevered pace. We are glad to play these little games, thankful that such small delusions are enough to deflect the world when we cannot stomach it.

Letta Mbulu, who was forced to leave South Africa in 1965 due to the horrors of apartheid, did not have the benefit of engaging in these deflections whenever she pleased. The land and life she left behind were never far from the music she made during her period of exile, but in "Normalizo"* Mbulu manages to declare that these forces which hold so many in thrall can actually be harnessed, used to confront the world and keep one's self above it.

Inuring the folk-leaning forms of her homeland with boogie, R & B, and a drumbeat that calmly unfurls to the border of proto-trap, "Normalizo" follows a woman of that name as she leaves her rural home in search of work in Johannesburg. A perfunctory whistle marks the opening, signaling that this sojourn is a necessity rather than a means of temporarily alleviating pressure. Despite the force of her person, a strength paralleled by the hypertrophied bass line that grounds the track, she is quickly disillusioned, with her hopes of something better met by a series of doors slammed in her face.

Normalizo turns to the past, a shift announced by the chorus switching to Zulu, South Africa's

---

*The reason *In the Music, the Village Never Ends* was a holy grail record until it was blessedly reissued by Be With Records, the indispensible UK label, in 2015.

most widely spoken indigenous language. She finds her footing. Her pace picks up, and when she looks upon the world it is now with clear eyes, for she can see through the refined facade to "a time when this whole land was a village."

This is not the gloss-ridden chunking that plagues most hindsight. Instead, it is a recognition that the present world is not, despite its insistence to the contrary, guided by a superior truth. The song turns triumphant as she sees that the harmony that allowed "loving eyes" to inhabit every face and made "every man a brother," has been replaced by the deceitful glittering surfaces of the "golden city / Where life is tricky."

When this verse is done, Mbulu and her band return to that unified past, falling into a spirited call-and-response. As their voices beseech the return of "that old-time feeling," it is clear that Normalizo, and Mbulu, want it back not because it is less complicated, but because it is simply more. More honest. More caring. Richer.

AKA THE MOTHERLAND

A few more testaments that Africa's musicians have always supplied the world's heartbeat.

Black Soul
Mangous Ye
Soukous / 1975

Look for the 12" mix that came out on Beam Junction in 1976, where the genius of Tom Moulton is on full display—extending the loping drum breaks and animating chants, excising just enough of the saxophone to ensure that it supplies rather than drains energy.

Oby Onyioha
Enjoy Your Life
Time / 1981

Onyioha's unruffled voice—amidst jaunty strings, a bass line so melodic it may as well get a vocal credit, and a glittering groove on the guitar—grants this track the backbone to serve as one of music's best kiss-offs.

Ozo
Anambra
DJM Records / 1976

With the Sanskrit mantra, "Om mani padme hum" intoned over bells, bongos, Pranayamic percussion, and ancestral chants, "Anambra" hypnotizes us long before we can wonder what this ritual intends.

Oscar Sulley
Bukom Mashie
Soundway / 2004 (Recorded 1973)

The galloping percussion, swinging bass line, and mambo-soaked horns that crowd the first three minutes threaten to drive you right out of your mind. When Sulley starts exclaiming in his spirited croak, you realize that fear was more than justified.

MAKERS
DON'T CHALLENGE ME
Midney / 1972

Timeless, yet indisputably way ahead of its time. With the cool and instantly familiar vocal, squiggly bits, abrupt changes in energy, and woozy groove, "Don't Challenge Me" sounds like something J Dilla could have produced—only it came out in 1972, more than 20 years before Dilla unleashed his innovative aesthetic.

Even though we have caught up, it remains easy to imagine folks encountering "Don't Challenge Me" over the radio and scurrying to switch it off, thinking some other dimension was attempting to reach out. It resides in the chasm between the classical music Makers architect Boris Midney started his career making and the disco he found success with—there is something inhuman in the unhurried tumble of vocal, guitar, synthesizer, and snare drum, something aggressive in Midney's use of space. We can't decide if the lack of urgency is contemptuous or indifferent, whether this is simply another path through the labyrinth, or a revelation that it contains additional levels.

JUNGLE BROTHERS
TRIBE VIBES
Warner Bros. Records / 1989

They are the Richard McDonald, the Steve Wozniak, the trailblazer pushed to the side by the machinations of history. The Jungle Brothers were the first member of the Native Tongues collective to release an album, the first to record a hit, the first to articulate that "conscious but ready to party" vibe that carried the other members, including A Tribe Called Quest, De La Soul, and Queen Latifah, into the pantheon.

What kept the Jungle Brothers from joining them is a case study in how circumstances and context carry, even for those who have "arrived." In 1988, their hip-house hit "I'll House You," brought them to the attention of Warner Bros., who had no understanding of how to market hip hop, or what to expect from it. When the group's next release, *Done by the Forces of Nature*, sold only 350,000 copies in 1989, it did not matter that the album was a clear step up from the work that had caused Warner Bros. to sign them, so lively and vivid that it can safely be slotted beside *3 Feet High and Rising* (De La Soul) and *Paid In Full* (Eric B. & Rakim) as one of the high points of late '80s hip-hop. It didn't matter that the album didn't even sell poorly by hip-hop standards at the time. What mattered is that it sold poorly according to the standards of a Warner Bros. artist. In failing to hit the metrics required at that level, the Jungle Brothers' promotion was written off as a mistake, and the group never found their way back.

The vitality of "Tribe Vibes" is what frames that oversight as an injustice. Featuring a muscular groove that runs circles around the tightly rolled, trap-inflected beats that came to dominate, it is a stark reminder of the time when hip hop was a movement rather than an institution. The house influence that eventually carried the JBs too close to the sun is also present, with the panning on the carefully deployed tambourine serving up highs that brush against the rarefied air of Adonis's "No Way Back." Most of all, "Tribe Vibes" possesses the combination of freshness and erudition that made the Native Tongues sound revolutionary. It is a meal thrown together by a three-star chef, with each component standing as a revelation. What it reveals, with its exhilarating references to the Blackbyrds and the Bee Gees, is a view of hip hop as a contemporary form of oral tradition, a way to transmit information between generations, and to ensure the vitality these forms carried in the past is felt by the future.

MARIE LYONS
SEE AND DON'T SEE
DeLuxe / 1970

After releasing *Soul Fever*, her remarkably assured debut, Marie Lyons disappeared. Featuring moments where she manages to be as bawdy and brassy as Betty Davis, as furious and despondent as anyone this side of Etta, the album should have gained her entry into the soul pantheon. But *Soul Fever* quickly drifted away, and Lyons followed, resurfacing in the late '70s in her hometown of Ashtabula, Ohio, as the owner of Queenie's, a bar she continues to operate. In the one recent profile I can find, she talks of her time in the music industry, of the Beatles sitting front row at one of her shows in New York during the '60s. But she makes no mention of what drove her away.

Listen to "See and Don't See." Lyons knows exactly how good she is and what she deserves. But she has not received it, and, frankly, she is tired. On its face, this song is about a relationship ending and the difficulty of managing the ensuing heartbreak. But as you sink into it, respond to the words and her tone, she could easily be describing the struggle of African American life. Or the indignities she has had to suffer because she was born a woman. Lyons brings all of this to bear in a vocal that resides between snarl and howl, carries the anger and aggression of a boot in the stomach. She is striking back, perhaps thinking that confronting the world with the contempt it has shown her will bring her some measure of respect.

Ashtabula is about a day's drive from where I live, and I've imagined myself making it. Arriving at Queenie's for the tail end of happy hour and watching Lyons as she presides over a place of her making, a place where her station and word can never be ignored or diminished. I have no idea if that's what Queenie's is. But my hope is strong enough to keep me well clear of it.

IMPERCEPTIBLE AND IMPERISHABLE

Little is known about the artists responsible for these exquisite instances of soul, which have taken on a life all their own.

Patti Jo
Make Me Believe in You
Wand / 1973

Just 17 at the time of recording, Patti Jo's ice-cold take on Diana Ross's smooth style is so accomplished we actually end up being thankful that Curtis Mayfield, who penned and produced the track, stayed off the mic.

Poncho C. Saint Fingers
When I Come Knocking
Greasy Records / 1980

Sure, the name seems like something a teenager who's decided to build his entire identity around pot would come up with. If you can manage to overlook it, you'll discover that Poncho was too busy beating Hall & Oates at their own game to bother with branding.

Calender
Comin' On Strong
Pi Kappa Records / 1976

Even amid the outlandish funk of their album
It's a Monster, this one stands out. The opening
heaves like a ship in stormy seas, merrily tossing
us back and forth between a guitar and shaker.
By the time the horns and flute descend, with
equal force, we're ready to accept whatever
may come.

Leo's Sunshipp
Give Me the Sunshine
Lyon's Record Co. / 1978

Spangled funk on the acoustic guitar, pulpy drums, and slightly harried strings fashion a groove just cool enough to keep the song's suggestive meteorological metaphors from becoming intemperate.

THE FANTASY
SUMMER NIGHT IN HARLEM
Secret Mixes Fixes / 2012

The song that, to paraphrase Theo Parrish (see page 153), "changed my DNA."

"Summer Night in Harlem" is an edit, a reworking of a song that extends or emphasizes an element or elements to release potential unrealized in the original. Although it is a simple rearrangement of a song I knew, Bill Withers's "Harlem," it did not feel simple the first time I heard it. In an instant, I realized that the world I'd dreamed of did in fact exist, that the one I'd been passively consuming was as moribund as it felt. I recognized, immediately, that a large part of my disillusionment was the speed with which I moved on from anything that was not perfectly consonant to who I wanted to become. It grabbed me by the throat and insisted the world was there to be shaped—that the true work was not waiting for spaces where you fit to reveal themselves, but to engage the world with such avidity that it became an excess of opportunities to create them yourself.

The rearrangers responsible for "Summer Night" are Brendan M. Gillen and Scott Zacharias, two central figures behind the Detroit underground retaining its vaunted status. Their rework picks up the pace from the version that appears on Withers's debut, *Just As I Am*, moving the snare and bass up front to transform the amble on the guitar that kicks off the original into a galvanizing stomp. This continues for a full minute, a massive build that Gillen and Zacharias deftly leaven, unfurling the gentle strings and extending them with a zeal that sends the head back, the eyes skyward, and grants the avuncular quality of Withers's voice an authority descended from on high.

LION
YOU'VE GOT A WOMAN
Philips / 1975

Imagine someone taking the bowl of sugary glaze the Bee Gees coated their songs in and inviting everyone to dig right in, instead of carefully applying it. "You've Got a Woman" has that kind of mischievous delight, the kind of indulgence you only allow yourself when someone new has made pain and discomfort seem impossible. Layers of syncopated drums echo the impatience to air what is rippling through us. The reggae-taut guitar has energy to spare. We bask in the sunbeam of Glenn Robles's falsetto. The bass carries the wonky kick of a bad sci-fi movie made unforgettable by the gleeful, snarky savaging we give it.

This 1975 collaboration between Dutch superproducer Hans van Hemert, drummer Peter de Leeuwe, and Robles was stowed away on the B side of Lion's only release, a 7". It remained hidden to those outside the Music From Memory orbit—where co-owner Abel Nagengast's edit was regularly driving people out of their minds—until 2017, when indie darlings Whitney released a cover that is deferential enough to testify to the power of what Lion had built, and too self-aware to attain the extravagance pulsing through the original.

PASTOR T. L. BARRETT
LIKE A SHIP
Mt. Zion Gospel Productions / 1971

T. L. Barrett's work as a pastor helped improve economic and social conditions for many in Chicago, and made him a leading light of that city's African American community. This prominence also enabled Barrett to defraud more than 1,500 people in various pyramid schemes. To avoid prison, he was forced by an Illinois court to remit the title to his church as restitution.

That offense is all the information some will need regarding "Like a Ship," proof that it intends only to deceive. Others will consider it separately, opting for the more forgiving view that a period of corruption does not mean everything an individual ever did is rife with it.

I incline toward the sympathetic stance. In light of what's to come, the song's uplifted, "blind but now I see" arc does not seem like a ploy building toward something nefarious. Instead, it speaks to the relief felt by a man who has at last come upon something that can keep him from yielding to the worst aspects of his character.

Barrett's arrangement is what gets me to believe. He turns what should be the song's bottom—the bass—into the enlightened, exhilarated piece, a brilliant inversion that carries the force of a personal epiphany. He counters this, and highlights the thinness of the line he is towing, by taking the bright innocence of a youth choir and making it sound weary, haunted by a knowledge they cannot possibly possess. The Youth for Christ Choir's responses to Barrett's reflections sound like the desert feels when it rains: every living thing is exalting, but the ecstasy feels tied more to the days of misery being past than the glory of this new state. They do not sound alive, but glad not to be dead.

YOU'VE NEVER HEARD YOUR FAVORITE SONG

What "Like a Ship" makes clear is that Barrett had hold of something powerful. That he ultimately proved unable to handle that power seems more human than it does wicked.

THE VOICE OF GOD

Lapsed, agnostic, atheist, whatever—these divinely inspired tunes render one's personal feelings regarding the spiritual world irrelevant.

Joubert Singers
Stand on the Word
Next Plateau Records / 1985

There is nothing quite like the journey from the opening's delicate piano and welcoming "oooohs" to the joyous tempest sucking up everything in its path waiting at the end. Larry Levan, the DJ who made the Paradise Garage feel like a sacred space for so many, is frequently, and erroneously, credited as the one responsible for its best-known mix.

Roger Rodier
My Spirit's Calling
Columbia / 1972

Wan guitar, hesitant, scoured vocals, graceful strings, and an unplaceable, otherworldly sound outline the levels of despondency that would cause one to believe a higher plane was reaching out.

Robert Vanderbilt and the
Foundation of Souls
A Message Especially from God
Sensational Records / 1978

The sumptuous soul of Manchild's "Especially for
You" is dubbed down into a solemn plea for us
to recognize that nothing but a glimmer of hope
remains. A song that could easily occupy the
anchor spot on a playlist intended to get Eddie
Hazel into the headspace required to play his
"Maggot Brain" solo.

Constance Demby
Om Mani Padme Hum
Gandarva / 1978

Granted a newfound appreciation for silence
by her yoga practice, Demby channeled that
epiphany into this atmospheric marvel off her
debut, *Skies Above Skies*, using very little—piano,
voices as tenuous as cirrus, and auspicious
synths—to carve out a massive space.

MC SHAN
THE BRIDGE
Bridge Records / 1986

His name no longer rings out, but this will give you some idea of Marley Marl's place in the hip-hop hierarchy: he invented sampling. The force of his discovery, the understanding that the world has been laid at his feet, resonate through "The Bridge." Following an enfilade of snares whose concussions charmingly throw the high hats out of whack, Marley and his cousin MC Shan announce that their home, New York's Queensbridge housing project, is no longer at the fringes of civilization, but the center of it. The pair sound as though they are in a huge, empty arena. They need an emissary to introduce them, and later to remind people who they are. They also sound entirely undaunted by these realities: they know hordes are on the way, and get busy drumming their origin story—a tale of misfits exiled to the wilderness, where they patiently lay the foundation for what will become a great empire—into everyone within earshot.

Considering that Big Daddy Kane, Tragedy Khadafi, Mobb Deep, and Nas came to call Queensbridge home, and what hip hop has come to mean to popular music, that hubris was not unwarranted. It also did not go unpunished: KRS-One and Boogie Down Productions—furious that somewhere other than the Bronx was being positioned as the birthplace of hip hop—boosted Marley's enchanted drum reel and used it on their career-making, and game-changing, diss track "The Bridge Is Over."

GOODY GOODY
IT LOOKS LIKE LOVE
Atlantic / 1978

For many who lived through the late '70s, disco is in the same league as the aquatic rabbit that attacked Jimmy Carter: emblematic of a culture at its nadir. That disdain is an heirloom at this point. It doesn't matter that the best disco records followed the same formula that fueled The Stooges—find a groove and don't let go— and were produced by people who are more interested in melody than marketing. What matters is that disco is a little too physical, a little too joyful to get those who inherited this healthy contempt to reconsider it. Plainly, it does not feel like it has enough substance to be worthy of review.

I would argue that anything gleefully ignored by a culture that could promote reality television stars through its ranks is fertile ground for discovery. The embargo has sapped the power of a music whose origin story carries the grassroots allure of folk and hip hop, the two genres that rose out of the underground and permanently altered the musical and cultural landscape. Distilling soul and funk to bring their dynamic rhythms to the fore, disco's rise was built upon a decade-long conquest of small rooms filled with people longing for a comfortable space away from the pain of life in a world that appeared to be faltering. That it proved unable to bear the weight of the pop music crown doesn't vaporize what occurred in those rooms, nor what those people felt.

"It Looks Like Love" is a portal into that world, proof that those who felt uplifted by disco weren't simply sucked in by some vapid formula. Written and arranged by Vincent Montana, Jr., one of the key players in the formulation of the majestic "Philly Sound," the song is executed with a grace and musicality that makes it as refreshing as it is decadent. Cutting against the track's supple bass line, Montana is liberal with the light touches he learned at the knee of Kenny Gamble, Leon Huff, and Thom Bell: a seductive flute in the intro; a raft of august strings; Chic-styled guitar; a whispery vocal that never stops echoing in the listener's head; a delicate run on the Fender Rhodes that evokes the cool tones of Milt Jackson's work with the Modern Jazz Quartet. These spiral down to the break, which is a master class in groove building. "It Looks Like Love" is disco at its liveliest, the work of individuals brave enough to follow the bold paths the music points them toward, knowing that all they need is a few people willing to let them through.

IT'S A BETTER THAN GOOD TIME

A few more opportunities to let disco's sunshine in.

Dinosaur
Kiss Me Again
Sire / 1979

Bouncing, jarring, and bursting with ideas. The genius of this uneven, Arthur Russell–helmed track (fun fact: David Byrne is on guitar) isn't fully apparent until the vocal in the second verse. The minute Myriam Valle sings "The door is unlocked, the windows are open," we are in for good.

Brenda Russell
Way Back When
A&M Records / 1979

The flamboyant complexity of a show tune and Russell's warm, walked-down vocal make this capable of melting through the steeliest grey.

Mary Clark
Take Me I'm Yours
La Shawn / 1980

The widest path through the crowded thicket that is producer Patrick Adams's legacy. Focused, ecstatic, and just unorthodox enough to catch every ear in range, an original pressing of 200 records is the only thing keeping this from its rightful place on the list of all-time greatest wedding songs.

Queen Yahna
Ain't It Time
P&P Records / 1976

This is no slight to the empowering stomp of Yahna's vocal, but I always gravitate toward the instrumental, which has the raucous, stitched-up texture of something Moodymann would cook up.

WHEN THE PAST WAS PRESENT: FOLK AND ROCK

THE ROCHES
HAMMOND SONG
Warner Bros. Records / 1979

Initially, we're for the sister who yearns for more, who is trying to escape the cloister of the family and follow her heart. We want to believe the warnings the other two issue are motivated by jealousy and pettiness, attempts to instill the fear that stymied their own quests. But as they keep at it, we recognize, the world being what it is, that they are probably correct: this lark is almost certain to do damage. They are only doing what you do with the people you love: try to shield them from pain.

As our loyalties vacillate, we become aware of the incredible tensions inherent in the structure of every family, an essential friction between an individual's desire to expand and be exposed to the world and the group's wish to contain and protect. This conflict has been integrated so thoroughly that no one bothers to notice that it is insuperable—everyone involved is able to feel singled out for particularly cruel treatment. The sisters' plea for the intrepid one to remain is both a complete disregard for her and a natural extension of the love that enabled her to feel capable of pursuing such a reverie. It does not feel like those things can both be true. The tragedy is that they frequently have to be.

It is the type of reckoning that only the best art can reveal, and it no doubt helps that the Roches are three sisters—Maggie, Terre, and Suzzy—who chose to acknowledge what they were born into and make their way together. The power of that decision is palpable in "Hammond Song." For an epic, there is not much to it: a guitar line that would be comfortable in a café or on a sidewalk, a triangle chiming in the back, some atmospheric noodling from producer Robert Fripp* in the bridge, and their three voices. And there does not need to be. At the end of the third verse, the sister who longs to go gives ("we fall apart") what she thinks is her final goodbye. Her concluding note carries into the chorus, a massive clash of forces that seemingly has to cause the splintering she desires and her sisters fear. But, as their voices swell, the world is revealed to be more elastic than we think, capable of a heartbreaking clemency.

---

*Considering his reputation, Fripp's decisions to produce The Roches' self-titled debut by "not interfering with the performance," and to recognize that there was no need to put his own stamp on the record are as impressive as his work as the mastermind behind King Crimson, the "Heroes" guitar solo, and his ambient experiments with Brian Eno in the early '70s.

JOHANNA BILLING
THIS IS HOW WE WALK ON THE MOON (IT'S CLEARING UP AGAIN)
Apparent Extent / 2008

Think of the opening cello riff as music's answer to "Call me Ishmael." Brief but sprawling, startling yet intimate. It is as fitting for the drive home from a first date with someone you are certain you will marry as it is for the minute after you watch that person walk away for the last time. Crushing and beautiful, it is an affirmation of what we know but, blessedly, allow ourselves to lose sight of: heartbreak is inherent in the hope we require to keep going.

That cello belongs to Arthur Russell, the apex of a career filled with powerful moments. Spanning disco, classical, and the space between folk and indie, Russell's work possesses a tender fearlessness that makes it seem uniquely attuned to the way life feels on the nervous system, and captures the full weight our thoughts and emotions, no matter how light, inchoate, or ridiculous, carry while within. When he is at his best, a Russell song is a comforting hand on the back, the closest thing the adult world can have to a lullaby.

But Russell's best-known recording of "This Is How We Walk on the Moon"* doesn't match the promise of his emotionally bowed beginning. His vocal gets shorted out in the middle of the song, a dissonance that seems more the result of a malfunction than experimentation. The song builds to make way for a trumpet that, though charming, sounds slightly chintzy following the lofty opening. The intensely personal nature of his work necessarily means that many of Russell's songs feel like sketches, vagaries to be fleshed out by sympathetic listeners. "This Is How We Walk" is too powerful a statement

---

*Which appears on the essential *Another Thought* retrospective, released in 2013 by Arc Light Editions.

to rely on the method Russell uses to foster that dialogue.

Johanna Billing, a Swedish conceptual artist, was so taken by the sound of Russell's song and the heartening sentiment of the title that she elected to use it as a framing device for her short film of the same name, which was released in 2007. Billing's facility as a filmmaker will forever remain a mystery to me, because her skills as an arranger are impeccable. Russell's transcendent cello piece is slowed and extended in space for nearly three minutes. The bongo, so peppy in the original, is ginger here, representative of the timid manner such strong feeling engenders. Scraps of dusky guitar send our mind over the land to a distant horizon. The trumpet is replaced by the pleasant, sun-drunk yawn of a melodica. Most important, that vocal Russell forgot out in the rain is recast as a duet for male and female, a fitting realization of the galvanizing effect the cello carries.

THAT'S THE WAY

Taking on a beloved tune is an easy way to curry favor with an audience. These covers go a little further, supplanting what seemed unassailable.

Idris Muhammad
House of the Rising Sun
Kudu / 1976

Bob Dylan stole this tune from Dave Van Ronk, and then Eric Burdon and the Animals rendered that dispute obsolete with their version. Muhammad, a drummer frequently employed by Pharoah Sanders and Ahmad Jamal, outdoes them all in this up-tempo, horn-soaked rendition that shows New Orleans, the song's spiritual home, the proper respect.

Susan Christie
Ghost Riders in the Sky
Finders Keepers Records / 2006

Deft fingerpicking, strong, lazy snare hits, and a vocal as wide and distant as a prairie skyline make Christie's version of one of country music's most-recorded songs—and Johnny Cash's biggest hits—the one that deserves to be considered canonical.

Jose Feliciano
California Dreamin'
RCA Victor / 1968

By quieting down The Mamas and the Papas'
massive original, Feliciano gets at the song's
somber heart, unmoored spirituality, and intense
yearning, while sacrificing none of its beauty.

Junior Parker
Tomorrow Never Knows
Capitol Records / 1970

The bombast has been stripped away in this version of the Beatles' psychedelic masterpiece, but Parker's deep, deliberate vocal still, and soberly, realizes its mind-altering potential.

Róisín Murphy
Ancora Tu
Vinyl Factory / 2014

Murphy takes her time in this rework of the
upbeat and heartfelt hit from Italian icon Lucio
Battisti, making it seem as though she is a world
away from the machined rhythm. What results is
a window into her breathtaking artistry.

TERRY CALLIER
SPIN SPIN SPIN
Prestige / 1966

The misfortunes that befall the immensely talented are often due to the volatile nature that attends human genius, the demons occupying the other side of the blessed coin.

But art's expansion into the popular sphere has introduced another group of unfortunates: those who possess such facility that they never develop the singular focus the market demands. Able to float between the interests that catch their fancy and unfortunate enough to be able to pull each of them off, they end up generating a diverse and far-ranging body of work that demands careful consideration, rather than a concentrated and quickly consumable product.

Terry Callier is a member of this hapless bunch, as his ability to move effortlessly between folk, soul, and jazz made him a difficult concern in a business where bankability and instant connection are guiding principles. Callier's only chart success was 1979's "Sign of the Times" and even that was far from massive, reaching #78 on the R & B chart. Callier found it so difficult to get any traction that by 1983 he had left music behind, took up computer programming, and eventually landed a data entry job at the University of Chicago.

That retreat into anonymity seems impossible the moment you put on "Spin Spin Spin." A lot of songs I connect with while digging remind me of stuff I've heard elsewhere—from whole songs to bass lines, hooks, and horn arrangements. These new discoveries become beloved by breathing new life into forms that have grown stale from overexposure. Encountering "Spin Spin Spin" was different, in that I'd never heard anything like it.

The song gestures at eternity—not heaven but the yawning void that reaches out in our loneliest moments—possessing all of the beauty and terrible power one would expect of such an artifact. You can picture a Cormac McCarthy character breaking into it as he stares into a fire that seems the only light in the world.

The instrumentation is sparse, but Callier's full, haunting vocal and the cyclic quality of lyrics that instruct a "little darlin'" to spin, turn, and dance fashion it into something considerable, so that you cannot help but be awed and slightly creeped out by it. Though not in the leering sense commonly associated with that term. "Spin Spin Spin" is creepy in the way a perfectly choreographed dance is creepy—so beautiful and uncanny that it seems unrelated to anything you are, articulating something you simultaneously desire and fear.

JUDY RODERICK
TWO HOBOES
Vanguard / 1965

There is a subtle difference between a song about sadness and a sad song. The former is what we turn to when the world collapses, the wreckage caging us in with our malformed thoughts. Songs about sadness assure us it is quite all right that our eyes are permanently clouded by tears. "Two Hoboes" is one of those songs that lifts this veil, forces us to realize that indulging our feelings in this manner, while valid, is a luxury. It is one of those songs that presents the world with stunning clarity, allows us to see those structures that will never collapse, and the people trapped within.

Judy Roderick pulls this off by carving a niche between the folk and blues traditions, proceeding with a lack of vanity and sentiment that enables her to hit every note square on the head and boldly trace the bleak outlines of the individual lives rendered in "Two Hoboes." Carrying on just above a tumbling acoustic guitar, we recognize that Roderick is not pondering them from a remove. She is seeing through their eyes, a radical bit of empathy that fixes our own vision. Seeing it, we cannot avert our gaze, shake our head, and move on, as we so often do. We confront, when she rolls through the lament that "when you're broke they all [every town] look the same," the privation that would grant one's perspective this austerity.

Roderick did not write the song. Dick Weissman—who contributed guitar and liner notes to *Woman Blue,* the album it appears on—did, reworking a recording the ethnomusicologist Lawrence Gellert made while traveling through the South during the 1930s. But it is all hers, informed by a vision so acute that a mystery of Roderick's own life seems to come into focus: perhaps her career was not commensurate with her talent because she could see through to all of the nonsense that would have attended this "success."

WILLOW
EVENING
20th Century Records / 1973

I am typically against all claims for the good old days. But the past decade has made it hard to turn on the radio without feeling that the muses have withdrawn to some inaccessible remove.

"Evening" opened my eyes to the desolation. The song's beauty would stand out in any age, but its craft, calm, and range sound particularly bright in the darkness of the current day, when, as James Murphy points out on LCD Soundsystem's "Tonite," every artist is acting like it's the last night on Earth. "Evening," sights firmly set on eternity, is gorgeous: layers of acoustic guitars, some gently plucked, some stroked until they ring; lush harmonies; and strings so tender they quiver. It is intelligent, featuring a poetic and pained chorus about the unsteadiness that comes once the sun goes down, managing to bring one of Hemingway's best lines to mind: "It is awfully easy to be hard-boiled about everything in the daytime, but at night it is another thing." Most important, it is restrained. The assurance with which Willow moves through the enormous space "Evening" inhabits is a far cry from the grasping maximalism of today. They understand that highlighting the emptiness in what they have carved out is far better suited to their purpose than cramming all they are capable of into it. They coolly swap one big piece—the ringing guitar, strings, and harmonies—out for another, framing the song as a series of assertions and retreats that mirror the internal dynamics of pursuing an elusive love.

Hearing it, I assumed a series of misfortunes unknown outside of Greek tragedy must have befallen the members of Willow for them, and this song, to slip into obscurity. But "Evening" can only seem that definite now, when the possibilities for a pop song have been winnowed to what will fit within a metric, when the most important audience is a collection of algorithms that crave the quantifiable.

MARIAH
SHINZO NO TOBIRA
Better Days / 1983

Its simplicity would charm a child. The autumn-flecked melancholy and dreaminess are consonant to the ambivalence of adolescence. The enigmatic vocal and bizarre juxtaposition of folk and new wave serve us well as we attempt to define ourselves through what we believe to be cool. The anxious gulp of the bass matches our response when the world bears down in middle age, the beauty and meditative quality providing the escape we crave as a result. And as we turn toward the end and sort through all that has passed, we appreciate its lighthearted brand of nostalgia.

"Shinzo No Tobira" is one of those rare pieces of art that can meet us at each stage of life, that is rich enough to retain its power as what we require evolves.* The song's guileless, repetitive rhythm is a testament to the daring of Mariah's leader, Yasuaki Shimizu, indicating his acceptance of the childish inflexibility that must attend serious play. This humility holds his bold theories—that the past can be melded with the future, that the provincial can be made unanimous—and predilections for new wave, techno, classical, ambient, jazz, and dream pop together, and makes "Shinzo" feel like the decisive moment in a great artist's development: when they acknowledge that their feverish ambitions may exceed their facility, that they are in fact incapable of judging their own competency. Shimizu's capacity to be uplifted by this loss of control is what ends up leaving space for our various incarnations to find a home.

Not that we would bother to without Julie Fowell's vocal. As weightless and exhilarating as a bird drafting on a thermal, her warm

---

*J. D. Salinger's "The Laughing Man" and the animated feature *The Triplets of Belleville* are other good examples.

interpretation of this strange blend of Armenian and Japanese is what will pull us back, guide us over the new terrain, ensure that Shimizu's plentiful and substantial ideas are never mistaken for instructions.

LOST IN TRANSLATION

It makes perfect sense that Japan's unique and rabid consumer culture would foster incredible pop music—but the rest of the world is only starting to realize the magic it has been piling in its vaults since the '60s.

Yukihiro Takahashi
Drip Dry Eyes
Alfa / 1981

As if Trevor Horn and Mark Hollis teamed up to compose a theme for a John Hughes movie. Charmingly bizarre, melodramatic, and with just a touch of ennui, it brings to mind someone shambling around an apartment, searching for something they hold a vague memory of but do not in fact have.

Gu
Marianne
URC / 1970

A whirlwind tour of Paris, Brazil, and Hawaii
concludes at a Japanese tea ceremony in the
middle of a dewy grove. In our worn-down state,
the familiar and calm is what feels exotic, and
worthy of commemorating.

Kyoko Furuya
Harumi Futoh
Better Days / 1982

Commencing with a zephyr of Hendrix-y feedback and quickly moving to a brassy vocal and drums that sound knackered from the continual beatings they're subjected to, "Harumi Futoh" feels like the best outtake from Blondie's peak. This track alone is worth the price of Chee Shimizu's *More Better Days* compilation CD. It may even be worth the price of having a CD player installed in your car.

Takashi Toyoda
Snow
Sound of Tranquility / 1985

Combining the dark ambience of Popol Vuh's scores for Werner Herzog with the transcendent loops of Tangerine Dream, it only sounds like a communication from another world: according to Toyoda, the song was produced by converting "biofeedback" from brain waves into musical notation.

ABU TALIB
BLOOD OF AN AMERICAN
Genesis II / 1974

It is telling that this song, one of the few products of the anti-Vietnam War movement that remains stirring, came with no cameras present, and received little to no attention upon release. Composed by a man compelled to act after one member of his band was killed in action and another entered the service, "Blood of an American" languished in obscurity for 34 years, until Melodies International reissued it in 2018.

Talib, who was then known as Bobby Wright, got that much-deserved day in the sun by managing to encompass the horror of the war and the disturbing glee of the antiwar movement. He steers clear of any rhetoric and homes in on the distressing nature of life in a world that is more concerned with ideas and supremacy than the obvious suffering taking place. It is an indictment, but by refusing to single out a villain, it is difficult for anyone who encounters Talib's quavering voice to consider themselves blameless.

Using only that voice, a guitar, and a bass, Talib wrote a song that resonates far beyond the moment that inspired it, allowing everyone who has ever felt oppressed by the American system to feel like there is someone who recognizes the desperation of being a pawn in its hostile games. Everything orbits around Talib, even the bass, which, initially, feels haphazard. But as his woe draws us in, we recognize the uneven rhythm of a heart under severe strain, at times just managing to go on, at times zooming ahead. This wavering rhythm also emphasizes the absence of drums. Despite everything Talib accomplishes here, this proscription is particularly poignant, a shrewd identification that their close tie to humanity's bellicose history leaves them no place in this benevolent plea.

MAXINE FUNKE
WHITE BIRDS
Epic Sweep / 2012

"White Birds" takes place in a space that is a cross between a confessional booth and a barely used parlor—it is cozy, but not warm. After a few soft pleasantries about the look of the day, Funke slowly recognizes and unpacks what is responsible for the doleful roil of the guitar running underneath. When she bends the song toward this hushed place and reveals the beautiful but inscrutable impressions that have been sequestered there—an ocean of jade walls is a particularly striking one—we cannot help wondering if the song was ever meant to extend this far. It feels personal in the extreme, intended as nothing more than a way for the creator to access her interior. We end up feeling more like an intruder than an observer.

This vantage is also rare enough that we can't turn away. We remain, telling ourselves we might learn something important. Funke is too surreal, too subjective to encourage such a dialectic. Near the end, she sprinkles a layer of weighty notes on top of the guitar's dismal burble, signaling that she's grasped what the matter is. Not that she's resolved it. In leaving things undone Funke finally makes herself understood: the escape, rather than the intimacy, is what drives her to this refuge.

BAS JAN
WALTON ON THE NAZE
Lost Map Records / 2018

The creative force behind Bas Jan, Serafina Steer, said she had never heard of Bas Jan Ader when onetime member Jenny Moore suggested the name. In 1975, Ader, a Dutch conceptual artist, set out from Chatham, Massachusetts, intending to sail across the Atlantic. He was never seen or heard from again. In his disappearance, Ader became a legend, patron saint to all those who wish they could commit so completely to the outlandish things inside of them.

The adrift, remote quality of "Walton on the Naze," suggests Steer quickly fell under the influence of that now mythic journey. Her vocal and insouciant bass line evoke those pleasant days when your brain is not quite operating well enough to tolerate indolence. When movement, though halting and lackadaisical, becomes essential to function. Those days when simply procuring a meal or a cup of coffee feels triumphant. Infusing Sibylle Baier's melancholic, confessional tone with the pluck of Françoise Hardy, Steer presents the song's narrator as the kind of person who could soft-pedal their way into anyone's heart, an individual so captivating she can make a leftover pickle sound enchanting. But as we draw closer, we find something lurking beneath this robust nonchalance, and discover that "Walton" has the understated quality of the very best fiction.

Set in the titular English resort town, the story's details are so unremarkable that they can seem worthy of narrative only for someone who has marked that day as a turning point, before everything went to pieces. Kicking off the song with the aforementioned gherkin heralds a pervading sourness, and it remains in the narrator's fridge not because of her blithe manner, but because it is the final vestige of her happiness. The seemingly delightful acknowledgment of brattiness in her desire for a present becomes just another manifestation of a neediness that eventually wore thin. The Hells Angels tranquilly sunbathing are not a symbol of how pleasant the day was, but of doom circling her and her partner. The dinghy her partner goes to see about is now seen as a life raft, the narrator's initial reluctance to go along signaling her obliviousness to the decayed state of the relationship. That enchanting ability to lend vividness to her surroundings is in fact available only in hindsight, making her no different than the majority of us. In the moment, she was simply floating along, barely paying attention, convinced nothing could ever go awry.

IT'S A FINE DAY

Not good, not bad. A few songs for those days filled with false starts, managing to highlight that there is something beautiful about the in-between.

Operating Theatre
Eighties Rampwalk
Cache Cache / 2012

Pulled from a radio session featuring this Irish theater company, the instrumental's solemn ebbs and delicate chiming carry the quiet anticipation of a scene where a character sits in silence in a meticulously outfitted room, determinedly stirring a cup of tea for one full minute.

Lucinda Chua
Feel Something
Self-Released / 2019

A startling revelation that Chua's voice is capable of matching her stirring work on the cello. It brings to mind souls looking in at the world, longing for an opportunity to leave the tranquil realm that holds them and experience what they've spent eternity observing.

Blueboy
Clearer
Sarah Records / 1991

Somewhere between Slowdive and early Belle
and Sebastian, Blueboy's vital role in '90s British
indie pop is coming into focus thanks to recent
reissues of *The Bank of England*, *If Wishes
Were Horses*, and *Unisex* by Australian label A
Colourful Storm.

Carlos Maria Trindade & Nuno Canavarro
Blu Terra
União Lisboa / 1991

Imagine, after a day laboring in the cold, sitting before a roaring woodstove and drinking a restorative broth from a bowl of unfired clay. "Blu Terra" carries the severity, grace, and surprising subtle touches that transform the modest into something unforgettable.

MICHAEL HEAD & THE RED ELASTIC BAND
PICASSO
Violette Records / 2017

The galloping intro. The ominous reverb on the guitar, prefiguring a showdown. The singer's weary, wizened voice. Hearing it all come together, you fully expect Michael Head to look down from the vast rubble of his life and tell us how things really are.

Thankfully, Head remains far too alive and self-effacing to settle for the view from that wretched peak. The lyrics of "Picasso" reveal someone who is certain only that the world will surprise him, who eagerly shuffles along, waiting for it to do so. Here, chance comes in the guise of a "pretty señorita," who Head falls for after observing her chatting on a telephone. When his pursuit leads nowhere, he concedes that "the movies" had some share in his overly optimistic projection. But the possibility that "there may be police involved" is the shock that truly opens his eyes, and lets us know what is behind the exquisite misdirection in the opening: the culture has acquired so much mass that we can't help traveling down the paths its narratives have etched in our minds, and we will notice this lack of autonomy only when disoriented, and vulnerable.

Although we may be increasingly constrained, Head has constructed a beautiful cage, a more refined version of the baroque pop he made as the leader of The Pale Fountains* in the '80s. Beneath Head's withered voice is the vestige of a ragged surf guitar. After the quiet reckoning reached in the chorus, a cello nudges us to ponder what has passed. A wild, eerie cry gives us pause as we bumble along. In the outro, a

---

*The 2013 Pale Fountains compilation *Something on My Mind*, and the catalog of the label it was released on, Les Disques Du Crépuscule, are both worth pawing through.

saxophone arrives to provide some needed levity, a wink that reminds us this is just one man's opinion. Given the weighty subject and quality of the components, most artists would slow everything down and space it out, ensure the extraordinary nature of what they'd captured really hits home. Head lets it pour out of him, sounding as hollowed out and unfiltered as a good friend calling from the road at three in the morning, hoping conversation will keep them awake because the gallon of coffee has ceased to. "Picasso" is that intimate, that uneven, that memorable.

WOO
IT'S LOVE
Cloud Nine Music / 1990

They speak the truth: the affectionate ring of "It's Love" sounds exactly how you hope someone looks at you after you've spent 25 years together. Its lighthearted, concise reverie conveys that this look has nothing to do with desire, or admiration, that these have more to do with ego than intimacy. In the guitar's elliptical lines, we find that instead it carries comfort, acceptance, tenderness—a tacit willingness to provide what is needed for another to flourish.

The conditions "It's Love" was created under offer some clue as to how something so powerful can be captured so serenely. Woo is the musical project of two brothers, Mark and Clive Ives, who have been diligently recording in their London apartments since the '70s, amassing an archive estimated to contain more than 1,500 songs. Restricted to guitar, woodwinds, electronics, and basic percussion by aptitude, space, and finances, and to a sociable decibel level by their proximity to others, it is only natural that their work would sound pacific, cosseted. The surprising force in that softness springs from the relationship between the two brothers, their innate attachment and unwavering commitment to collaboration granting them access to one of the laws that rules the universe: when two things share a frequency, the sum is necessarily greater than the parts.

I WOKE UP NAKED, ON THE BEACH, IN IBIZA

Before it became the glitterati's party destination, Ibiza was a quiet island that gradually pulled in the world's strays and gave them the space to forge a peaceful, goofy, earnest sound all their own: Balearic. The boundaries are fittingly permissive—so long as it suits the sunset, it's in.

Jonathan Jeremiah
Happiness
Quiet Village Remix
Rosario Records / 2009

Adding cinematic strings, breaking waves, and a little delay to Jeremiah's soulful vocal, Quiet Village cram a two-week vacation's worth of escape into this remix. For something a little more upbeat and fleshed out, Metro Area's Morgan Geist also has a wonderful take on the song.

Sandro Perri
Love and Light
Tom Croose Remix
Phonica Records / 2012

At first, you can almost see the waitstaff walking around lighting tea lights, hear the oars turning through the water in a nearby harbor. From there, Croose deftly layers an array of halting fragments from the original until the song is the only thing getting through.

Lena d'Agua
Tao
CBS / 1986

Portugal's d'Agua turns to the East here, breezing us through a perfectly manicured garden where the center is always a little farther on than we expect, allowing the hope that we are stuck there forever to rise.

Guru Guru
Taoma
Brain / 1979

The krautrock pioneers took a detour from their psychedelic stylings in the late '70s and ended up stumbling upon this opulent, sax-and-synth soaked gem. An outpost in the slightly cheesy territory Balearic is more than willing to annex to keep the good vibes flowing.

ADRIANO CELENTANO
PRISENCOLINENSINAINCIUSOL
Clan Celentano / 1972

So taken with the sound of American slang that a complete lack of fluency did not seem like a barrier, "Prisencolinensinainciusol" finds Italian superstar Adriano Celentano gleefully spouting gibberish in an attempt to mimic what he heard. Such an approach should consign the song to novelty status. But between a fuzzy, snarling guitar, cocksure horns, a harmonica solo that reminds us of the whimsy this oft-somber instrument is capable of, and a beat that sounds like John Bonham playing the world's largest kick drum in a stone cathedral, Celentano's glossolalic ramblings are perfectly in line with the song's infectious energy.

While "Prisencolinensinainciusol" can ignite an all-night party, Celentano's willful ignorance and eager embrace of absurdity did not prevent him from outlining something essential to the American experience. His rap carries the familiar timbre of the sales pitch, that slick aggression that is so effective at preventing people from recognizing when they are being taken for a ride. He understands, implicitly, that in a country where little escapes marketing's clutches, how something makes people feel is far more important than what is actually being said.

ANGELO & EIGHTEEN
FLIGHT 2
RAK / 1972

Picture someone injecting amphetamines into the opening of "Sympathy for the Devil," believing that they could actually summon the dark lord with it. Between a nasally howl that sounds like a mind reveling in its disintegration and a no-holds-barred beat that is reminiscent of Walter Gibbons's work in the late '70s, "Flight 2" possesses that measure of dark, hallucinatory frenzy.

Had Angelo Finaldi and Richard Tate stuck with this souped-up primitivism, they'd still be dining out on their legacy. As it is, I imagine that they recorded it as a goof, tossed it on the B side of their only single as a dare, and happily returned to their careers as hired guns for artists like Peter Noone of Herman's Hermits and Nanette Workman. They must have been pleasantly surprised when it showed up on *Songs for the*

Dog & Duck, a 2009 mix CD curated by the famed music nerds in Saint Etienne, and downright stunned by the mark their precocious mixture of aggression, break beat, and subby bass leaves on everyone who encounters the track.

FLOATING POINTS
KELSO DUNES
Pluto / 2017

Sam Shepherd, who produces under the name
Floating Points, seems like the product of some
covert government program designed to prove
that people actually can achieve whatever they
set their mind to. In his early 30s, Shepherd has
composed exceptional work in genres ranging
from jazz and ambient to dance and rock, become
one of the world's most sought-after DJs, and
headed two respected labels, all while picking
up a PhD in neuroscience and epigenetics at
University College London.

While it is tempting to wonder what Shepherd
could have done musically had the academic
world not consumed so much of his time,
the openness of "Kelso Dunes" suggests
Shepherd's hours in the lab were crucial to his
artistic development, fostering a comfort with
experimentation that cuts against his uber-

achiever wiring. An impromptu recording made outside in the jagged calm of Joshua Tree, Shepherd lifts an idea from one of his personal favorites—Azimuth's "The Tunnel"—and fashions a tight swirl on the synthesizer as two guitars ping off the surrounding rocks. They hold each other in that vastness, gaining momentum until we can feel the force of all the wind that has gone into sculpting their surroundings and see the sheared-off bits tumble over the land, a reminder that this desolation is constantly expanding.

NO JOY
GHOST BLONDE
Mexican Summer / 2010

Shoegaze has become something of a dirty word, though not because the music is so obviously objectionable that those who fall under its spell feel duped later on. Instead, the derision the genre elicits is tied to its various expressions being as agreeable and individually unmemorable as a grilled cheese: we pleasantly nod along as we consume it, and then never think about it again until another opportunity pops up.

"Ghost Blonde" has the same ingredients as the genre's other space holders: vocals low in the mix, crushing amounts of feedback, a swirl of heavily distorted guitars. But the auspicious, sleigh bell–styled percussion signals that something is different here, spiriting the track along as the pressure builds beneath the haze. Eventually, it blows a hole in the thick wall of sound, a spurt of intensity that transforms the song's droning into something danceable. "Ghost Blonde" does not wash over you. It lifts you, buoys you. By the end, we don't want the vocals up in the mix because we are desperate to locate a song amid all this sound. We want them up because we sense that this is a band with something valuable to say.

ERASMO CARLOS
VIDA ANTIGA
Polydor / 1972

Another example of early success hindering the evolution of an individual. The same box that sent Dylan into a ditch cast Erasmo Carlos into darkness the moment he tried to defy expectation and articulate what was inside of him. After coming to prominence in the '60s as part of the bubblegum set featured on Brazil's popular television program *Jovem Garda*, Carlos drastically changed course in the '70s. The resulting blend of rock, samba, soul, bossa nova, funk, and folk attained a quality that many assumed to be impossible given his lightweight reputation, and was duly ignored.

"Vida Antiga" beautifully captures the nature of this plight. Carlos is weary, but his vocal retains the charm that captivated Brazil in his youth. He cannot, despite his fatigue, help it. He sounds far from the microphone, granting his voice the stature he feels is his due, while also acknowledging that he is held back from inhabiting it. The bright rhythms of the instrumentation, carried by the musicians who would go on to form the massively influential jazz-funk trio Azymuth, occupy the foreground. It is pleasant, drenched in sunshine, but also pointed—Carlos asserting that, in his own life, the music has always come before everything else.

DON'T STOP THE DANCE

The fluidity, style, and sensuality that inform the world's mythic conception of Brazil are most evident in its wide-ranging, lively, and expertly crafted music. Many would be perfectly happy spending their lives sifting through nothing other than what its tradition has produced.

O Terno
Eu Vou
Risco / 2019

The swirl of feelings that would attend a walk during magic hour at the height of fall. We are astounded, but also held back from becoming absorbed by an awareness that all of it will soon vanish. A song that exalts and laments in equal measure.

Cassiano
Onda
Polydor / 1976

A swampy bass line, vocals that carry the optimism, longing, and innocence of puppy love, and brilliantly underplayed horns float you through an impossibly effortless eight minutes that share a wavelength with what Marvin got into during "I Want You" and "A Funky Space Reincarnation."

Burnier & Cartier
Mirandolina
RCA Victor / 1974

The epitome of locked in, with slight hitches that make this smooth and lissome piece of jazz feel like a series of jubilant outbursts. After a few listens, you recognize just how many musicians are putting all their might into making it seem like they're not there, thrilled at the freedom they've found in unanimity.

Os Tincoãs
Jó
RCA Camden / 1975

You could go with any track off their devastatingly breezy *O Africanto dos Tincoãs*, but this funky combination of Nick Drake–styled folk and Cuban jazz is the warmest welcome into the catalog of a band that never seems to take a wrong step.

SYNESTHESIA: ELECTRONIC, JAZZ, AND CLASSICAL

OH, YOKO
SEASHORE
SPRINKLES' AMBIENT
BALLROOM
Normal Cookie / 2012

The club is a strange place for a philosopher to hang a shingle. It is a place that aims beyond the intellect. A place with the rare power to interrupt the narrative loop that binds consciousness together, leaving a blessed void only the body is capable of inhabiting.

Yet it is one of the spaces artist and essayist Terre Thaemlitz, who produces under that name, as well as DJ Sprinkles, Kami-Sakunobe House Explosion, and a number of others, has chosen to air her views on capitalism, gender, sexuality, race, and the effects of technology. One goal of her work, Thaemlitz says, is to help those seeking release "keep sight of the things [they're] trying to momentarily escape from."

An antagonism that only her deft touch for arranging allows her to pursue. In her rework of "Seashore" Thaemlitz maintains the effortless quality of the original—a charming, melancholy amalgam of coos, aimless guitar strumming, and wobbly piano—with a lush yet simple beat that also manages to transform the offhandedness into something operatic. Pinwheeling through the dense atmosphere is the voice of Gil Scott-Heron, a sample that has been twisted until "balling" becomes the far more suitable "falling."

And then, aware of the escalation the club has conditioned everyone to expect, Thaemlitz tears down her delicate construction. The beat evaporates, ceding the floor to a heartfelt speech where one man assures another that the world has a place for him. But the address, which one could almost picture Atticus Finch making were it not quite so on the nose, turns out to be from one of those insipid police procedurals that rule network TV. The individual it is directed at is a gay man whose partner just killed his ex. In this context, the words become those of a politician—superficially about hope and togetherness, actually focused on self-interest. The speech is not there to console anyone who shares the addressee's sexuality or feelings of alienation, but to scoop up those audience members who know enough not to be titillated by these "others," though not so much that they care if that identity is used to drive ratings, and sell cars.

A level below this knotty piece, we discover why Scott-Heron received so much weight in the opening movement. Thaemlitz zooms out on the "balling" sample to show that it is contained within a song where Scott-Heron, celebrated champion of the marginalized, strikes his famously strident tone while unleashing the chilling hate of "The Subject Was Faggots" from his debut album. It is the language of frat boys screaming at each other late on a Saturday night. In coming upon such blatant ignorance in that setting, we would know how to respond, and could remain remote as we express our shock and disapproval. To discover it coming so casually from an artist renowned for intelligence and compassion directs the condemnation inward, forces us to speculate on the cost of our own cluelessness.

Underneath these eye-opening asides, barely audible, is the tender intro for Bronski Beat's "Smalltown Boy," an anthem for the gay community in Berlin. With lyrics that tell a tale of the hostility, bullying, abuse, and exodus that are common features of adolescence for homosexuals, and anyone ever accused of being different, the song endures as a haven for the ostracized.

By the time the beat returns, we've completely forgotten about the transcendent promise of the opening. Precisely as Thaemlitz, convinced that the focus on tension and release has necessarily left little room for the dynamics that gave birth to the club, intended. Populated by marginalized individuals seeking shelter from a world consistently hostile to their very being, in those early days the dance floor was the center of the conversations and exchanges that make a community. It was a place where people came not to escape the trappings of identity, but to celebrate and nurture each individual.

In trying to spirit us back to that time, Thaemlitz achieves something rare in electronic, or any, music: she manages to captivate while also keeping our gaze firmly on the world that looms outside of the song. By stepping away from the tension-release tug-of-war, she gets us to recognize the ephemeral nature of our consolations, and reminds us that, instead of continually fleeing, we should think to turn to one another.

BARNT
WHAT IS A NUMBER,
THAT A MAN MAY KNOW IT?
Magazine / 2010

In the beginning, there is only a low, mysterious thrum, a sound so monotonous and indifferent it appears to have been occasioned by a yawn. Something begins hammering upon it, insignificant in comparison, but incessant. This bit of fidgeting gets the ether to churn, spawning massive pressures that are expressed in a series of labored exhales. Eventually, a beam of light works its way out of the darkness, confirming the suspicion that we've been eavesdropping on the birth of the universe.

With that two-minute display of force and elegance, "What Is a Number" becomes a red pill, a rabbit hole, fostering awe and suspicion of the very things that underpin our reality and also allow us to transform it. To voice all that flashes into the mind during this pursuit would threaten one's place in society. But the sense of an earnest intention behind the generous access we have been granted to the far-ranging power of numbers becomes undeniable and unsettling.

Since the song's release in 2010, Barnt has become known for cartoonishly brutal tracks like "Geffen," "Chappell," and "If She Says She Is a Healer, She Is a Healer." Both mocking the prevailing humorlessness of the techno community and disquieting listeners with their machined guilelessness, they seem like songs Michael Rother and Klaus Dinger of Neu! might have produced had they grown up worshipping Aphex Twin instead of The Kinks.

"What Is a Number" is plastic where these are concrete, the product of a vision rather than a perspective. Although obviously modern, it channels something ancient, reminds us that the miraculous does not lie in particulars, but in those shadowy forces that allow them to take shape, to be beheld by us. Its ponderous, abstract beauty slips us into an atavistic state where the extraordinary does not uplift, but terrifies, insists that you will always remain outside, small, impotent, and misinformed.

HE SAID
PUMP
Mute / 1986

Its calm is unnerving. Its celebration of the obvious cultivates anxiety over what is about to be revealed. The subtle drama in "Pump" is the work of Wire bassist and lyricist Graham Lewis, who fleshes out the lively minimalism he and his bandmates are known for in this lavish celebration of dissolution.

A humid bass line, decayed claps, and Lewis's conversational baritone provide a stage for the Shakespearean fool to stand upon, offering observations that easily can be ignored, but always at our own peril. We know that "Grass doesn't grow on busy streets," as the song's first line tells us. Lewis's pacing and his hissing of each sibilance make us doubt ourselves, wonder what more could be here. He dwells in a back corner of an opium den, either conferring wisdom that would be very costly to draw from experience, or initiating us into a life of depravity. Its murk maps new territory, connecting the burrows of Depeche Mode and Orchestral Manoeuvres in the Dark to the shadowlands Trent Reznor and Portishead would eventually occupy.

WHO'S THIS?

These artists are instantly recognizable, but the shadow cast by their best-known work forces these other gems to languish in obscurity.

The Beach Boys
'Til I Die
Alternate Mix
Capitol Records / 2000

The combination of melancholy, beauty, and space that Brian Wilson used to make *Pet Sounds* bulletproof reaches its apex on this existential hymn that is tucked away on the *Endless Harmony Soundtrack*, a compilation of previously unreleased material.

Carly Simon
Tranquillo
Elektra / 1978

I could have gone with 1982's "Why" in this
slot, the infectious result of her work with the
always-on-target Nile Rodgers. But the build to
the crescendo of strings and the range of Simon's
vocals in "Tranquillo" cry out for more, and
much-deserved, attention.

Little Richard
I Don't Know What You've Got
(But It's Got Me)
Vee Jay Records / 1965

Featuring two legends—a not-yet-incarnate Jimi Hendrix is the guitarist—and none of the pyrotechnics each are known for, this song is easy to overlook, despite Little Richard striking a wracked tone so persuasive that it has aged better than the souped-up tracks he built his career on.

Jimmy Page
Damask
Self-Released / 2012

Part of the soundtrack Kenneth Anger asked Page, fellow Crowleyite, to compose for *Lucifer Rising*. At some point, Anger turned his back on Page's project, electing to go with friend, and Manson family member, Bobby Beausoleil's score. Page's soundtrack was released in limited quantities in 2012, and its contorted, fearsome arabesques are freighted with the dark power that seemed to desert Page outside of Led Zeppelin.

Curtis Mayfield
Do Do Wap Is Strong in Here
Curtom / 1977

The rise of disco kept this bleak (a reference to
the devil and the horrors of prison life feature
in the lyrics) slice of funk from making the
impression it deserved in 1977, but it's one of
the finest moments in Mayfield's brilliant career.
Make sure you get the single version and not the
one that appeared on the soundtrack for the film
Short Eyes—the former is streamlined, giving the
song the punchiness it needs.

TAHITI 80
DARLIN' (ADAM & EVE SONG)
JOHN TALABOT OBSCURO
BAILE REMIX
Human Sounds / 2010

Giorgio Moroder, the "Father of Disco," opened a portal when he sequenced the bass line on "I Feel Love," the jaw-dropping precision that resulted enabling a speed and intensity previously unthinkable. What Moroder discovered was the musical equivalent of the wheel, an implement that could connect previously segregated lands.

But even a wheel is only a tool. For many, Moroder's innovation has become more than that. It has led to an astonishing amount of music that is, literally, breathtaking. But it has also removed some key element, something that allows a track to go deeper, do more than simply elicit the conditioned response from the nervous system.

John Talabot feels like one artist who has recognized this cost. On the whole, his tracks are slower and more delicate than those of his contemporaries, while still managing to match their grand scale. A machine could easily smooth the edges off the components he uses and make everything seem of a piece, but Talabot understands that this integrity is the artist's charge. To achieve it, he turns to sounds that will be natural to anyone who comes across them. Tree frogs, flutes, flamenco guitar, calmly struck percussion, and emotive vocals fill his songs, and Talabot carefully floats them amid synthetic elements until a massive, breathing composition results. The outcome is tracks like "So Will Be Now," "Matilda's Dream," and "Depak Ine" that are not simply hypnotic, but synesthetic—tracks whose physicality comes from within the listener, instead of a speaker.

Talabot's rework of "Darlin'" came toward the beginning of his quiet revolution, and as one would expect of someone in the throes of a powerful discovery, he made it entirely his. The original is fine but forgettable, something like Phoenix before Philippe Zdar's magical combination of playfulness and precision pulled them from the indie rabble, and lifted *Wolfgang Amadeus Phoenix* into the canon. From Tahiti 80's base, Talabot, determined to look for answers between the lines, seems interested only in what's contained within the title's parenthetical. A wooden beat and what sounds like one hand clapping with remarkable facility set a simple, placid scene. The beat picks up, the clapping hand gets a fervent partner, and a crystalline synth makes us picture the primordial couple, unconsciously delighting in their paradise.

The components, beautiful and shimmering as they are, are also fragile, untenable. There is a burgeoning curiosity as a ragged surf guitar riff and what sounds like a steel drum filled with the human voice join the fray, building energy until we arrive at the inevitable collapse. We hear a vocal, drowned in sorrow, and recognize it as what the conversation that came after the fall must have sounded like. When this is past, the song explodes, urgent and haunted, subtle layers being added with each passing bar, Eve's sorrowful plea looped into a baleful question that continues to echo today.

TRAUMPRINZ
2 BAD
DJ METATRON'S WHAT
IF MADNESS IS OUR
ONLY RELIEF MIX
Giegling / 2016

Ghostly techno as Prince of Denmark. Tribal polyrhythms as Prime Minister of Doom. Nostalgic house and ambient as Traumprinz and DJ Healer. Delicate trance and break beat as DJ Metatron. All the work of one man, all as excellent as he himself is mysterious. In this doggedly public age, he is allowed to remain anonymous because his tracks give listeners everything they need. They hold you as you sob, all alone in the center of a crowded dance floor.

"2 Bad" outlines what we would feel at the close of the period that David Bowie commenced in "Five Years": exhausted from the rush to cram experiences into our heads, rolling over as all of those moments we have gathered crack up and dissolve. When its yawning synths, deliberate, crackling beats, and Mary J. Blige vocal sample signaled the close of DJ Metatron's breathtaking *This Is Not* mix for the Giegling collective, it felt like a requiem. Experienced on its own, we see that "2 Bad" is not meant to foster acceptance. We are more than ready to be sucked into its void, relieved to encounter the oblivion that has been on the horizon for years.

FATIMA YAMAHA
WHAT'S A GIRL TO DO
D1 Recordings / 2004

When electronic music works, it can feel as though you are mainlining the emotions of the artist, actually feel the instants where catharsis occurs. It is not just the ability to convey feeling without words that fosters this sense. Classical music and cinema can also do that. It instead seems tied to the electrical devices that frame contemporary existence. We are predisposed to cutting through so much complication with the press of a button. Electronic music, because it is produced on instruments that enable a similar immediacy, is a form that can acknowledge this relationship and still provide the emotional calories we require from the art we consume.

"What's a Girl to Do" plays coy initially, starting with a chintzy beat and low-key vamp that a 10-year-old could fashion on a Casio keyboard. Considering the intensity of what is to come, it is a sharp incline that offers an escalator down, an artist's way of stressing that, if you are one who can confidently dismiss something an eighth of the way through, you are free to leave, because you could not possibly appreciate where the journey leads.

In an instant, thanks to a ponderous bass line, the song takes the shape of every afternoon you've spent hiding from the world, seized by uncertainty and inexplicable guilt, convinced some terrible force will descend at any moment. A winsome piece rises above this valley, not clearing away the dread, but providing it room to breathe. Like a pet or a long milkshake or a body of water at dusk, it has the power to make you feel understood in those moments where nothing reasonable is passing through you. You can't help but sing along, despite there being no words.

This reverie is interrupted by a meeting with another drifter, the Scarlett Johansson of *Lost in Translation*. She shrugs off our surprise, saying

"I just don't know what I'm supposed to be." She asks, "Does it get easier?" It will not, of course. But as she departs, a soft choral piece takes her place, just light enough to help you understand that you are not alone, but with yourself.

THEO PARRISH
SUMMERTIME IS HERE
Sound Signature / 1999

There's an interview with Terry Callier (see page 80) where he talks about going to see John Coltrane perform and actually being frightened by the intensity. Here was someone operating at the highest creative level, boldly proclaiming with each breath that treating music as a matter of life and death was the only way to access it. Every musician will say they want to attain the same level. Callier, himself never driven by the urgency that possessed Coltrane, recognized that no amount of talent could close the gap between himself and what was occurring on stage, and was rightfully concerned that he could not remain standing if he committed himself to the degree Coltrane did.

Theo Parrish resides at a similar crossroads, able to inspire or eviscerate simply through being. An encounter with his energy, acumen, daring, intelligence, and outlook could send young artists hurtling down their own path. The force of his person could also back those freighted with too much ego or uncertainty into a corner, harangue them until they determine they aren't _____ enough to accomplish what they claim to want.

Although he is categorized as a producer of house music, it would be more accurate to say that Parrish uses the methods traditional to house to make jazz, fusing live instrumentation, electronics, and samples into compositions containing so many vital ideas that they almost gasp. A typical Parrish track throbs with the grumbly, jagged, and gritty pieces most would file down, if not scrub altogether. But Parrish, whose ability to traverse genres and eras as a DJ communicates a lifetime of close listening, understands better than most that these bits are where the soul of a track lie, are the elements that lift a song from nice to unshakable.

"Summertime Is Here" is smoother than the slightly twitchy tunes that dominate his catalog.

It is the rare Parrish track that can sit in the background, that is not vehement in its demand for complete, sustained, and repeated attention.

But "Summertime" is too gorgeous and evocative to label as "Theo Light." Instead, it is to summer what Vince Guaraldi's *Peanuts* compositions are to Christmas: redolent with what makes the season magical, rather than exciting. A reminder that the heightened feeling we have for the season is not meant to foster perpetual motion, but to delight in the moment and discover the minuscule wonders residing in the outwardly simple. The comforting rumble of the kick drum, then, is the blessed sound of a thunderstorm after a string of oppressively humid days. The woozy cymbals a loved one's fingers on your neck, asking if you need another drink or anything before they head in. The horns and gaggle of voices the sound of the rushing city from a rooftop far enough away for the chaos to soften into a soothing harmony.

TORNADO WALLACE
TODAY
Running Back / 2017

A polestar for any artist eager to be swept along by what the internet has placed at their feet. Australian producer Tornado Wallace and vocalist Sui Zhen have the contemporary affinity for reference, but each allusion has been shaped until it bears the timeless and universal nature that carried these inspirations to them. They manage to inhabit the past and those places they look to, rather than simply pose against them.

The booming drums and digital clicks make one think: Brazil in the '80s. The lavish guitar and light atmospherics cause us to suspect that its origin is embedded in the experimental pop Japanese musicians began making in the '70s. Zhen's unaffected vocal shifts the scene to a German national who has expatriated to Bali and now spends her nights sitting below strings of café lights at a tranquil bar in the middle of a jungle. It is everywhere, and nowhere, unstuck in time, a ship that anchors but never disembarks. The title, then, is revealed to carry a tinge of irony: the current abundance of artifacts and the ease of accessing them threaten to turn the present into nothing more than a recollection of times and places other than our own.

LEON VYNEHALL
MIDNIGHT ON RAINBOW ROAD
Rush Hour / 2016

"Midnight on Rainbow Road" captures the one instance where the road's much-rhapsodized capacity to engender enlightenment is not off base: the middle of the night. It understands that there is something fundamentally unsettling about the speed at which the automobile sends us through time and space, an agitation that means we miss most of what passes by our window, see just enough for it to serve as a distraction. In the dark, this constant tugging at our senses disappears, forcing us inward.

Taking a lint brush to the fuzz-coated atmospheres My Bloody Valentine made famous, Leon Vynehall cuts through the haze that typically clouds our mental life, carves out a bit of space amid the world's perpetual shifting. A cascading guitar, indistinct voices, and clicking of a woodblock are just chilling enough to be refreshing, reviving us to where we can pay attention to the insight that exhaustion enables. The energy of the guitar picks up slightly at the end, a sign of the slight thrill that attends the successful navigation of a paradox: we are glad to be approaching our destination, and also to have this little bit of time away.

THE PROJECT CLUB
EL MAR Y LA LUNA
LOVEFINGERS REMIX
Is It Balearic? / 2011

As one of the world's leading crate diggers and head of the leftfield label ESP Institute, Lovefingers, aka Andrew Hogge, has used his impeccable taste and insatiable appetite for music to bring an unthinkable amount of tunes the larger audience they deserve. A small part of what makes his rework of "El Mar y La Luna" so lovely is its guarantee that people will one day do the same for a production of his.

"El Mar" is the musical equivalent of a microdose. Outwardly simple and privately byzantine, it ends up revealing one's own construction, with the song's currents assuming expressionistic shapes as they pass between your synapses. A driving acoustic guitar and loping percussion form that deceptively composed surface. If one can keep from drifting away, they'll find that the drums, through volume, angle of attack, and pace, extend in approximately 20 different directions, lending the track a sense of movement and space that would overwhelm us were it not for the pedal steel keening softly in the background. Instead of feeling besieged, we are awed to find that each piece is exactly where it should be.

ESCAPE FROM NEW YORK
FIRE IN MY HEART
Rollerball Records / 1984

One of many debts owed to DJ Harvey, who has used his proclivity for similarly overlooked, gaudy tracks to fashion what is regularly referred to as "the world's greatest party," Mercury Rising at Pikes Hotel in Ibiza. Through his unapologetic embrace of excess, one comes to recognize that some tracks remain underground because they are Too Much Fun to be aired in any situation where even a trace of uptightness is present.

In "Fire in My Heart" that looseness comes from a band that changed its name (from the Orwellian-inspired Airstrip One) and decided to indulge every sound they'd pretended to hate in order to maintain their post-punk bona fides. There's the dubbed-out, buxom rhythms Francois Kevorkian popularized with his mixes of Yaz's "Situation" and Dinosaur L's "Go Bang," the raw energy of electro, the synthetized funk of late Bill Withers, and the go-for-broke vocals of Italo disco. All of this is cast into a Moroccan souk at night, where someone lovely and alive catches our eye and then meets our gaze, setting any practical considerations alight, encouraging us to pursue what we actually want.

RUNNING UP THAT HILL

Reagan, painful displays of tone-deafness, and an instantly dated aesthetic tend to paper over the reality that the 1980s were music's best decade.

Paraf
Napunjeno Vrijeme
Helidon / 1984

Evolving from their role as punk progenitors in Croatia, Paraf went full-on Goth—the ones who sacked Rome, not those who think platinum-selling artists are edgy—in this doomed, tribal-inflected slice of dark wave.

The Reels
Return
K-Tel / 1982

The Reels, who sat on the crest of Australian new wave, capture the brief surge that attends the resolutions and discoveries arrived at early in the morning, when they seem to be the remedy for every ailment that has held you back. Nothing may come of them, but "Return" understands that sitting and plotting the conquests these magic bullets will enable is its own kind of industry.

Mirage
Woman
Crash / 1983

One of the high-water marks of Italo disco, where artists didn't let limited resources (ability and taste usually among the lacunae) hold them back from doggedly pursuing the epic. When it is right, as it is here, its amalgam of house, electro, Euro pop, and video game score is as exhilarating as a midnight ride down a highway during a new moon with your lights off.

Steady B
Don't Disturb This Groove
Jive / 1987

By snatching numerous pieces of the Headhunters' unassailable "God Make Me Funky" and riding Steady's amiable rhythms, this snippet of Philly hip hop manages to hit hard while feeling as light and irresistible as a circuit on a merry-go-round.

BULGARIAN STATE RADIO & TELEVISION FEMALE VOCAL CHOIR
KALIMANKOU DENKOU
4AD / 1986

"If it moves me, it'll move other people." According to 4AD founder Ivo Watts-Russell, the decision to license *Le Mystère des Voix Bulgares* (*The Mystery of Bulgarian Voices*), the album "Kalimankou Denkou" appears on, was that simple. Knowing nothing more than what he'd heard—not even the title, "Prïtourïtze Planinata"—Watts-Russell nonetheless heeded the call and eventually tracked down Swiss ethnomusicologist Marcel Cellier, who had recorded the choir on trips to Bulgaria during the 1950s, somehow managing to repeatedly maneuver around the strictures of the Iron Curtain.

It is easy to see why both men felt so compelled. "Kalimankou Denkou," featuring soloist Yanka Rupkina, is opera that has been attained, rather than executed: art made by people who have had so little exposure that they can only turn within, explore what the human voice is capable of. There is far more dissonance here than heard in other choral music, a quality that grants the song a palpable sense of struggle—the harmonies have been dragged to their feet rather than offered from on high, forcing one to stand at attention and wonder at the nature of the worlds contained in these women.

PLACEBO
BALEK
CBS / 1973

With a wonky, electronic loop dopplering
through the track, "Balek" sounds an alert that
the accepted limit of jazz is approaching. Marc
Moulin, the creative force behind Placebo,
responds by jubilantly punching the accelerator.
Moulin's early, eerie lines on the Moog resemble
a snake charmer's tune—he is playing with
something very dangerous, he believes proximity
to hazard is the only way to make the endeavor
feel worth it.

The song is oriented toward the future, but not
without reference. The flat crack of the snare
looks back to Sly Stone's "In Time." The daft
lines on the Moog dovetail with the bright solos
of bebop. The depth of Moulin's graceful work
on the Rhodes walks over the bridge Jimmy
Smith built between jazz and Motown. But
Moulin understands that the energy an influence

carries is what's holy about it, not its form. That energy can be spirited onward, used to forge new connections. The form can only be preserved, each act of maintenance helping it become a little more antiquated.

Moulin's graft of Stone's drum sound also happens to anticipate the sharpness of hip-hop. Those slightly glitchy, playful lines on the Moog point to the proto-techno he would make later on with Telex, and the electronic jazz he would make at the end of his career. The track's synthetic funk and rousing horns also shed light on a key piece of jazz's past: it started as dance music. It was meant to get people up and moving, not fix them in place. Subtly, devilishly, "Balek" is Moulin carrying on that tradition.

JOE PASS
A TIME FOR US
Discovery Records / 1969

Timing is everything. After spending the 1950s and early '60s either in prison or trying to get clean, Joe Pass turned to Synanon in Santa Monica, California, the first-ever self-help, no-doctor drug rehabilitation program. He remained two and a half years, and Synanon's unorthodox methods not only gave Pass the strength to overcome his heroin addiction, but the center also provided him a stage to show off his incredible talent—Pass's first solo record, *Sounds of Synanon*, featured him and his fellow patients.

After its release in 1962, Pass and Synanon went in entirely different directions. Instantly hailed as a star, Pass launched a career that saw him stand shoulder to shoulder with legends like Oscar Peterson, Count Basie, and Ella Fitzgerald, and won him a spot on any credible list of the all-time greatest jazz guitarists. Synanon devolved into a cult, and eventually dissolved when its founder, Charles Dederich, and two others were convicted of trying to kill an opponent by putting a rattlesnake, from which the rattle had been removed, in his mailbox.

Pass's ability to locate the sweet spot in an otherwise doomed situation carries on in "A Time for Us." Spirited, tempestuous, and brooding, it matches the atmosphere of America during the year it was released, 1969, serving as a testament to the unrelenting nature of the forces behind such moments of upheaval. In this surprising take on a song Shirley Bassey recorded in 1968, Pass trades the nimble lines he built his reputation upon for thicker, more considered chords, providing a poignant counterpoint to the enormous energy of the choir, which is propelled by the belief that they are destined to realize the beautiful world that has been established as an impossibility. Pass may sound stiffer than normal, but only because he is adroitly fulfilling his duties as The Man, enforcing the boundaries society requires to exist. His guitar lends the struggle a gravity that is painfully literal, dragging down that which would otherwise soar, coolly asserting its fundamental inescapability.

BEN COSGROVE
MONTREAL SONG
Self-Released / 2014

For a moment, we move softly, slowly. The world has taken a form we do not recognize. It maintains that it has been fashioned with you in mind, but in a foreign tongue. It is agreeable, beautiful, but so mysterious and unlikely that you approach cautiously, brow furrowed, mouth agape.

With recognition, and acceptance, momentum builds, allowing you to move at the thoughtless, breakneck pace you didn't realize you'd always craved. Suddenly, after years of settling and stumbling had carried you far from such enchanted spaces, you could not put a foot wrong if you tried. Each movement, each encounter, opens to an epiphany.

"Montreal Song" manages to sound like falling in love feels. The absurdity and beauty, exhilaration and surrender that attend it are all contained within, Cosgrove's considered tones and breathtaking runs on the piano personifying what a million painstakingly crafted verses have failed to.

An itinerant pianist whose constant travel grants him access to the various landscapes that inspire his compositions, Cosgrove's work tends to be both hermetic and expansive, possessing an air of solitude while also encouraging a closer look at the environment. "Montreal Song" sees him abandon the remove that his keen intellect and considerable talent allow him to operate from. He is still alone. He just isn't analyzing, or intent on conveying what is before him. For once, Cosgrove expands the frame to allow himself and what is happening within to appear. He has surrendered, allowed himself to be swept along, pulled toward something so new and so powerful that it still carries the possibility of being perfect.

GIDGE
I FELL IN LOVE
Atomnation / 2014

This is not a record of that glorious descent. Instead, "I Fell in Love" uses the past's preterite form—something completed, definitively concluded—to outline everything that comes after. Its delicate scratchings and dissonant rattles feel remote: rustlings interpreted through a wall or a door after a fight; someone doing the dishes, either as an escape from criticism or because they can't stand to be in the presence of the other. The gentle mist in the background is the fog of anger, exhaustion, and sorrow that distorts your perception. The vocal is warped by pain—each fissure in what was comes through with perfect clarity, everything else is incoherent. As things approach the end, it feels as though you are losing your mind. And you are. The mind that you have known, with so many of its thoughts and plans inclined toward this one person, will leave with them.

Tears that seem too large to fit inside a person begin to drop into the void. Hearing this, we pause. There is a bottom. A few rays of sun poke through. Our emotions swell, but are coherent at last. When this fades and the heartbreak returns, it is a little more intense. But we see it as the rush that follows an ice dam breaking up. A little less numb every moment, we become inured, able to recognize that this too will not last forever.

NILS FRAHM
SAYS
Erased Tapes Records / 2013

For a classically trained pianist who also worked as a sound technician, Nils Frahm has an autodidact's obsession with using limitation to expand what is possible. His 2011 album *Felt* saw him place that soft fabric in front of the piano's strings to dampen the sound. The music on *Screws*, his following album, was composed around a broken thumb he'd recently suffered. Such experiments help Frahm's work sound less reverent than one would expect from a pianist— he approaches the piano as a tool, rather than the altar it has become.

Frahm also struggles to read sheet music, an affliction that in his youth forced him to physically drill each piece into himself, one bar at a time. In "Says," he uses that comfort with repetition to float until he lands on something solid. When he does, each individual note gets his undivided attention, hastening a grandeur that seems impossible from his initial scuffling, while undeniably of a piece with it. Eventually, Frahm comes in so tight that the notes become visible for the listener as well, dropping like snowflakes against a streetlight, moving fast or slow, swirling or drifting straight down depending on what one chooses to focus on.

HARVEY MANDEL
CRISTO REDENTOR
Philips / 1969

Using a guitar, harp, and piano to simulate the light slowly filtering into the air, a trio of voices to suggest chittering birds and the calm they punctuate, and lilting strings to convey the lightness our activity will quickly bulk out, "Cristo Redentor" limns the glory in the momentary blankness of dawn, the only point of a day not colored by what we accrete as we move through the world.

Given the title, structuring the song as an evocation of the sunrise makes sense considering its long history as a symbol of redemption. But the song's halcyon beauty extends the metaphor beyond its Christian trappings of waywardness set right, back to a time when the appearance of first light was a refuge from the absolute terror of night, the darkness so complete that it rendered us powerless. Mandel, showing remarkable restraint for a 22-year-old guitarist, is at the center of this asylum. Although his controlled playing means he is constantly at risk of being swallowed up, this delicacy grants those moments when he rises up slightly a breathtaking power and purity.

GÁBOR SZABÓ
GALATEA'S GUITAR
Skye Records / 1968

Able to manipulate the guitar until it carried the sustained complaint of a horn or the potent grace of a stone skimming over water, Gábor Szabó managed to slide between genres and styles with such ease that it feels more accurate to say he conjured his unique sound rather than landed upon it. (There's a reason a 1967 live recording of his band is called *The Sorcerer*.)

"Galatea's Guitar" has the odd juxtapositions and aural sleight of hand one would expect of the album it kicks off, *Dreams*. It begins with a rippling, mournful riff from Szabó that sounds as much like a zither as a guitar. After a brief, pensive opening up, the track's sorrow is quickly repressed into a groove both sinister and seductive, with Szabó's guitar snaking around the piano, Latin percussion, and double bass. Powered by Szabó's peculiar logic, this section marries gypsy-style folk, calypso, and funk while conserving their unique shapes, surreptitiously building tension until the piece begins to feel menaced, and dissolves into a chaotic swirl marked by palsied stabs at a piano. Quickly, Szabó returns to the zitherlike notes of the opening to restore order, intuiting that the rest of us can only briefly tolerate the tumult that marked his interior world.

TARIKA BLUE
DREAMFLOWER
Chiaroscuro Records / 1977

Another vista provided by J Dilla's towering genius, as he molded the slinky, little-known groove of "Dreamflower" into the root of Erykah Badu's "Didn't Cha Know." That song's success (and a reissue funded by a settlement that was reached after Chiaroscuro Records called out the unlicensed usage) helped rescue Tarika Blue, a late '70s project from keyboardist and recording engineer Phil Clendeninn, from total obscurity.

A steady, muted bass and a brushed-on beat lend "Dreamflower" a steadiness that allows Clendeninn's smooth Fender Rhodes and mewling leads on the ARP Odyssey, languid guitar from fusion don Ryo Kawasaki, and Fred Miller's jaunty English horn to feel always on the verge of slipping away. This long leash underscores the power of the song's internal logic—it has embedded itself in each band member's brain, eliminating the struggle between subjectivity and sacrifice that can cause jazz to become distended or disjointed. In comparison, "Dreamflower" breezes along, guided by destiny rather than any determination. While this straightforwardness may not seem particularly hard to pull off, the impression "Dreamflower" leaves indicates that it is nearly impossible to do this well.

GRANDBROTHERS
EZRA WAS RIGHT
Film / 2014

The beginning's soft, absentminded tones are the eyes blinking open. The early sluggishness those ginger steps out to the kitchen. We brighten as the coffeemaker or the kettle runs its course, though still need the counter for ballast. That cup, its warmth, snaps things together, shifts the scene to someone who has labored on one piece for years and sits back, recognizing that it has finally clicked into place.

The unorthodox percussion and jubilant piano at the center of "Ezra Was Right" are that triumphant, carrying the wonder of a moment that decades have been skillfully balanced upon. The song is a pair of awakenings: one that we know, the other which we aspire to. Able to meet us where we are and tenderly point to where we wish to go, "Ezra" can distinguish a solitary walk at dusk as easily as it could capture the swell of a wedding entering the reception hall.

DISTILLED IDEAS
FOR CURIOUS MINDS

Curated to be useful, entertaining, and informative,
Curios range from cultural appraisals to culinary
guides, packing plenty of punch no matter the subject.

ACKNOWLEDGMENTS

Everyone involved in the creation of the preceding songs, and those who recognized their quality and felt moved to share them, thank you. I am forever in your debt.

Marena and the boys, thank you for putting up with everything attached to this madness, and for making every turn onto Loring feel like a triumph.

The crew in Tamworth, who sat around night after night and continually backed up my belief in the power of these songs, y'all are far better friends than anyone deserves.

Buzz Poole, who gently nudged each of these pieces into a much better place and never let me cheat, is a major reason why this is a book, and not a glorified playlist.

Lee—thanks for walking me down the long road to this point—I could not have done it without you.

ABOUT THE AUTHOR

Matthew Doucet is a writer and editor who lives in the foothills of New Hampshire's White Mountains. He spends his time trawling the internet for music and arguing with friends about things they don't know all that much about. He is also the author of the second entry in the Curio Series, *How to Talk Like You Know What You're Talking About.*

ABOUT CIDER MILL PRESS
BOOK PUBLISHERS

Good ideas ripen with time. From seed to harvest, Cider Mill Press brings fine reading, information, and entertainment together between the covers of its creatively crafted books. Our Cider Mill bears fruit twice a year, publishing a new crop of titles each spring and fall.

**BOOK
PUBLISHERS**

"Where Good Books Are Ready for Press"

Visit us online at
www.cidermillpress.com
or write to us at
PO Box 454
12 Spring St.
Kennebunkport, Maine 04046